BE BOLD
BE BRILLIANT
BE YOU

Lessons from the C-Suite to Accelerate Your Career

Katrina McGhee

This book is dedicated to all of the amazing professional women who are committed to making the world a better place. You inspire me.

THANKS AND LOVE

This book has been a labor of love that's been a long-time in the making. For nearly a decade I've been jotting down little nuggets of wisdom from my career. To be able to share them with you is truly a dream come true.

There have been so many people who helped me along my journey. I wish I could grab them all up in a great big hug and say thanks. But for now, I'll settle for expressing my gratitude on the page that precedes the work that they made possible by investing in me.

BE BOLD, BE BRILLIANT, BE YOU

As always, I start with my parents, Frank, Jr. and Patricia McGhee. They've been my constant throughout my career. It is their journey of going from picking cotton, to college, to vibrant careers, that inspires me the most.

To my son Brandon, thank you for supporting my dreams, even as you work to build your own. If you're a part of my Academy, it's his genius that allows us to work together, no matter where you're located. I am a very blessed Mom, which will always be the position I'm most proud.

I also want to say a special thank you to two of my bosses – Dennis Milne and Hala Moddelmog. I've been fortunate to serve under many great leaders but these two in particular allowed me to flourish into the person I am today. I am so grateful for you allowing me to spread my wings.

On a personal note, I want to thank Brandon's godparents, Torie and Willie Miles. Without them I would not have been able to be successful at home and at the office. They ensured my son was well loved, while I was away working on other priorities. I am so grateful for your love, friendship, and support.

To Brea Kratzert Todd, Julie Teer, Emily Callahan, Crystal King, and Hattie Hill, thank you for continuing to open doors to support my success, some of which I had no idea existed until you called. Your faith in my abilities is what inspires me to aspire higher.

Finally, to all the women and men who've allowed me to support their career journeys – thank you. Every time I speak, teach, or coach it's a privilege. Thank you for pouring into me, as I have poured into you.

BE BOLD, BE BRILLIANT, BE YOU

KATRINA MCGHEE

CONTENTS

THANKS AND LOVE 9

INTRODUCTION 15

EMBRACE YOUR SPACE FOR GREATNESS 21

ACTIVATE YOUR UNSTOPPABLE SUPERPOWER 41

SIGNAL YOUR SUCCESS READINESS 57

COMMUNICATE YOUR BRILLIANCE WITH CONFIDENCE 87

CULTIVATE YOUR CAN-DO CONNECTIONS 101

CREATE YOUR BALANCE WITH PAIN-FREE PRIORITIES . 123

SPREAD YOUR LOVE LIKE LIFE DEPENDS ON IT 137

THE ROAD AHEAD 149

ABOUT THE AUTHOR 155

MORE BY KATRINA MCGHEE 157

BE BOLD, BE BRILLIANT, BE YOU

INTRODUCTION

My life feels out of control. I want to be successful at home and at work. But lately...I don't seem to be doing a great job at either place.

I'm not sure I'm in the right role. I can do it, but I'm bored and I'm not growing. Surely there's got to be something more.

I'm ready to go to the next level, but my boss doesn't seem to think so. What do I have to do to get noticed and promoted?

Would it surprise you to know that the majority of

people are unsatisfied with their work experiences? It sounds like an exaggeration, and yet a recent Gallup Poll reveals that it's true. Eighty-five percent of people worldwide hate their jobs.[1]

Ugh! Statistics like that make me so sad, especially when I know we don't have to live that way.

> You can create a life you love, full of all the things that matter most to you. A career that is enjoyable, rewarding, and fulfilling is within your reach.

Yet even in places like the United States where opportunities abound, 70% of workers report feeling the same discontent. Why are we settling for less? More importantly, how can we break out of the mindset that this is all there is, and instead, pursue the more that life has in store?

As a speaker and career success strategist, I have the wonderful privilege of teaching and mentoring a plethora of professional women. They're smart, ambitious souls who have so much to contribute to the world. Yet I often find them disillusioned and frustrated.

Even those that enjoy the work they do are still dissatisfied with how they do it. They often ask what's the secret to...

Finding work/life balance?

Getting a mentor or sponsor?

Being true to myself and still fitting in at the office?

Having traveled the beautiful, nerve-wracking journey from individual contributor to chief marketing officer, I am intimately familiar with their angst. I know what it feels like to be overlooked, ignored, and discontent. I also have experienced the joy of growing past stalled and experiencing unimaginable success. I believe you can also.

My professional path was undoubtedly special but not an exclusive journey. There are thousands of women who have traveled well beyond their wildest dreams. Many of us were just like you when we started out – hungry for success, happiness, and significance, but not sure how to achieve it.

Through experience and insight gained from those a little further along the path, we found our way. We discovered the very best in ourselves and found joy in sharing it with the world. It's why I'm so passionate about taking this journey with you.

Here's one thing I know for sure -

> **When you understand who you are, what you want, and what you can uniquely contribute, success is your destiny.**

In this season of life, my work centers on preparing and positioning women to lead and succeed. I get so excited when I meet women who want to pursue a vibrant career, while also enjoying life, and supporting important causes.

I'll bet that sounds a lot like you, doesn't it?

Well, I've got some great news! By the time you finish this book you'll have a better understanding of what it takes to create the life you want to live, and to develop a professional path that gives you more of what matters most to you. You'll also have some insight into those "secrets" you've sensed you may be missing, and how to apply them in a way that affirms your value and worth, while also advancing your career.

Our first step is to focus on increasing your self-awareness. One of the most transformative experiences you will ever have is to define you for you. There is no greater joy than fully embracing the notion that who you are – your unique personality, gifts, and abilities – is enough.

Oh my goodness I am so excited for us to embark on our grand adventure. But before we do, let me tell you three quick things.

First, my approach to career success is rooted in empowered living. It's impossible to talk about how to create a career that is enjoyable, rewarding, and fulfilling without also addressing how to get in the driver's seat of your own life. As we journey together you will start to gain clarity about your priorities, choices, and natural next steps in both your personal and professional life. This is one of the most beautiful parts of our journey, as you learn to reconcile all the disparate parts of your life with your authentic you.

The second thing to note is that each lesson contains lots of practical applications that can immediately amplify your impact. In the shaded boxes are **bold** thoughts to challenge your long-held truths. The exercises are designed to illuminate what's **brilliant** about your divine design. And of course, throughout our time together we'll be learning more about what it means to be unstoppable **you**.

The book is designed as an exploratory journey. It's a quick read, but I challenge you not to rush to the end. Moments of reflection are when we often receive the most powerful revelation.

Finally, think of me as your navigator for the journey. I'll point you in the right direction and cheer you on, as you get behind the wheel and accelerate your career. I'm writing this book from the heart because I believe in you. Your hopes and dreams of a life you love are within reach. You have so much more power than you've imagined, and together we're going to get you ready to share your brilliance with the world.

Let's get you in position to shine.

LESSON ONE

EMBRACE YOUR SPACE FOR

GREATNESS

Want to know the key to your success? It's you. Your unique blend of gifts, skills, talents, and abilities, delivered with excellence at the right time and place, are the keys to creating the life and career you desire.

It sounds a little too simple to be true, right? After all, you've been showing up as "you" your whole life, and yet you still don't quite feel like you've hit your stride. What's the deal?

I discovered one of our chief challenges while recently speaking on a leadership tour. As part of my workshop I encouraged attendees to identify their areas of excellence by answering the following two questions.

What are your top 3 areas of expertise? For each area, what is a specific example you can share to highlight your excellence?

Once they had their responses they broke off in pairs and conducted mock interviews. Person A was the candidate. They had applied for an internal position and been selected for an interview. The role was a stretch, but they were ready for a new challenge.

Person B was the interviewer. Their job was to question the candidate on what they do best, seek out specific examples of when they rocked it, and then talk about how their skills could be applied elsewhere. At the end of the exercise, the interviewer provided feedback to the candidate on how they presented themselves, and how well their example highlighted their expertise.

I conducted the exercise in eleven different markets across the United States and Canada. In every city two things occurred.

First, most of the attendees were uncomfortable with identifying any of their skills as an "expertise." Some said it felt like bragging. Others said they weren't sure they were an "expert" at anything.

Second, many of the women in particular struggled to own their excellence. A common theme of the feedback was encouragement for the candidates to be more confident in sharing their story. It was a strange and consistent revelation. Even when the candidates knew that they had excelled, they struggled to pinpoint and articulate their specific contribution.

Watching this happen over and over helped me understand why so many of us are dissatisfied with our careers. Sadly, it's because we have not become intimately familiar with our own greatness. As a result, we never fully develop the confidence or the fulfillment that comes from knowing that we're offering the world our very best.

You see, most of us spend the majority of our time trying to shore up our weaknesses rather than build up our strengths. And hey, I get it. To be seen as less than competent in skills that are critical for your position can be the death nail in your career.

That's why when you identify areas of your performance that need improvement, be they soft skills or technical abilities, it's important that you take action immediately. Find a class or coach to increase your proficiency. Don't wait for your employer to provide professional development. Be proactive and get in the driver's seat of your own growth.

At the same time, don't lose sight of the importance of building upon your strengths. They, along with your skill set and experience, are what give you a unique expertise. Continue to develop your mastery by a) practicing your craft, b) staying current on trends and innovation in your industry, and c) plugging into a system that encourages ongoing learning. The most impactful way to increase your value and influence is to make a commitment to continuous improvement.

I want you to write the phrase below on a sticky and post it somewhere you can see it every day.

> Worrying over my weaknesses will never lead to greatness. It is only when I maximize my strengths that I can achieve unimaginable success.

Am I saying we can ignore our weaknesses? Absolutely not. What I'm suggesting is that worrying is a waste of time. If you're taking action like I suggested above, quit fixating on your weaknesses to the point that they are all you see.

Instead put them in proper perspective. First, stop calling them weaknesses and instead refer to them as areas of challenge. That immediately allows your brain to move from worry to work. Second, put a plan in place to improve, and then release yourself from constant rumination. There is no part of learning that requires beating yourself up in order to be better. Work your plan, and you will progress.

This approach will keep you out of hot water so you can focus the bulk of your energy on what you want – creating a career path you love.

The best strategy for beginning that adventure is to identify, and then intentionally inhabit, your **space for greatness**. That's the zone where you are unstoppable! In your space for greatness, you and others around you can easily identify your expertise because, you'll be known for consistently delivering excellence. You'll also be enjoying the journey.

Your space for greatness is where your brilliance shines brightest. It's where your strengths, skills, desires, and willing "to-do" align in a manner that allows you to operate from a position that brings out your very best. You'll feel good because you're clicking on all cylinders and as a result, you experience unimaginable success.

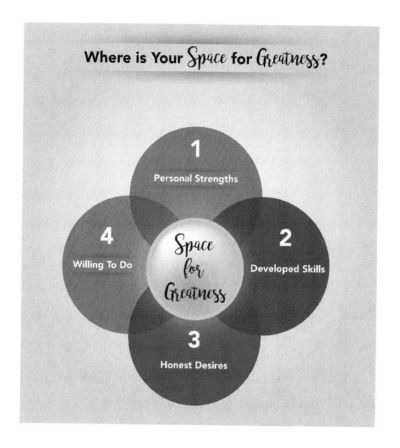

The great news is your space is not limited to a particular place or role. In any number of positions, you can achieve greatness, as long as all four of the key areas are in sync. Ask yourself the following questions to determine if the role you're currently in, or one you may be considering, is in your space for greatness.

1. Is this role rooted in my personal strengths?

Let's first determine if what you're naturally good at is critical to the success of the role. Or another way to think about is if I were designing an ideal job, based on my strengths, would I consider this position a viable option?

Assessing roles this way ensures that the strengths you bring to the table will be *invaluable* in your position. This is the first step in setting yourself up for success.

Now I know some of you may be struggling to identify your strengths. Don't be distressed. It's likely that between college and the early years of your career, you've already completed an assessment that highlights this information for you. If so, use that data to get you started.

If you don't have anything like that, use the questions below to jumpstart you in creating your own list.

What have I enjoyed doing since I was a kid?
What is it that I'm normally complimented for?

What is it that I feel naturally good at?

What accomplishments give me the most satisfaction?

Your answers should provide some insight. If they don't, I recommend that you Google "how to determine my strengths." A number of free online quizzes will pop up to give you some direction. If that's not enough, you can also purchase a more comprehensive strength assessment tool that will give you a full profile.

Whichever method you use, the goal is to get a clear picture of your strengths, so you can align them with your assignment.

2. Am I utilizing my most developed skills?

Unlike your strengths, which come naturally to you, skills are learned. You develop and master them through education and experience. When you find a role that fully embraces your unique blend of strengths, and the skills where you excel, you're one step closer to your space for greatness.

As you're considering whether a role is right for you, bear in mind that your strongest skills are usually those that emanate from your personal strengths. They are the ones that will allow you to deliver your very best and will bring you the most joy. Here's an example from my own life to illustrate why this is so important.

One of my personal strengths is communication. Ever since I was a little girl, I've been really good at connecting with people through stories. In fact, my first job was as a tour guide at a historical park. I was fourteen years old.

Now here's what's interesting. When they hired me, it was as a building monitor. I was stationed in this little one-room house built in the 1800s. My job was to make sure no one touched anything outside of the designated areas.

As you can imagine, after a few weeks of just sitting there, I got bored. I decided to liven things up by telling the visitors stories about a family who may have lived there. One day, as I was in the middle of my monologue, my boss walked in.

Y'all I was so nervous! I wasn't sure how he would feel about me sharing my made-up stories. But as it turns out, I had nothing to fear. When the guests left to go on to the next exhibit, he looked at me and said, "Congratulations. Next week you're going to start giving tours."

That was the first time in my life that I remember thinking, I'm pretty good at this. With no training and no experience, I had gotten my first promotion. All it took was surrendering to what came naturally to me.

Throughout high school, I enjoyed speaking so much that I sought out opportunities to do more of it. I even took a speech class to improve my skills. But when I got ready to go off to college, I never considered anything related to communication as a career. Instead I majored in computer science, and later switched to accounting. Things I was also good at seemed like a much better choice for a career.

I'm betting some of you can relate to this part of my story.

As a kid, maybe there was something you loved to do. It came naturally to you, but as you got older, it just didn't seem substantive enough for a career. You, your parents, or perhaps a guidance counselor decided that you needed to make a safer choice. So, you pursued something you were pretty good at and laid your budding excellence to the side.

It's a path many of us take and often live to

regret. That's because something inside of us is hard-wired to seek out our space for greatness. Those strengths we were born with were given to us for a reason, and the skills that emanate from them have a way of emerging, even when they aren't allowed to fully flourish in our current position.

This is another one of the reasons so many of us are discontent. Our skills are stifled. We're in roles that are made up of things we can do, but there's nothing about them that inspires or challenges us to work toward excellence. As a result, we have bursts of brilliance, but like so many of the candidates in our interview exercise, we don't dwell there long enough to become intimately familiar with our greatness.

That's what happened to me when I graduated college and got a job in accounting. I had the skills to do the work. There were even parts of it that I enjoyed. But there was nothing about the role that consistently brought out my highest and best. Like the people in the study I referenced at the beginning of the book, I eventually became discontent.

So, I got in the driver's seat of my career, and decided to make a change. While continuing to work

I went back to school part-time and got my MBA in marketing. Then, shortly after completing my studies I made a conscious choice to do things differently.

I started searching for a new position that would allow me to do what I loved and make a living. I didn't just want to be employed. I was on a mission to be engaged, to excel, and to enjoy my journey.

That's the position you want to be in, too.

If you want to create a career you love, you have to pursue a role that allows you to bring your strongest skills to the party. I'm not talking about things you "can do." I'm talking about the skills where you rock. When you put them into action your brilliance emerges in spectacular fashion. You feel good about your contributions, and as a result, you begin to seek out new avenues where you can give value.

3. Have you identified your honest desires?

There are a myriad of ways and places that you can use your expertise to make a difference. The key to operating in your space for greatness is to do more of what you are designed to do – based on your strengths and skills – and less of the things you may be proficient in, but don't really interest you.

This is not to say that you won't ever have to do things that you don't like. One of my least favorite tasks is administrative work. But as a small business owner, I have to stay organized. Every month I set aside a couple of days to focus exclusively on invoicing, expense reports, and general administration. I discipline myself so I can be fiscally responsible, and then I outsource the rest to a bookkeeper. My goal is to invest the bulk of my time and energy on responsibilities where I get the greatest return.

If you're committed to creating a career you love, that should be your goal, too.

Ideally you want to find a role that allows you to be brilliant and balanced. Believe it or not, both can be achieved while operating in your space for greatness. The key is to be honest with yourself about what you desire for your life and your career.

Here are some thought starters to help you clarify what matters most to you.

The most important thing in my life right now is...

I am happiest when I...

My ambition is to...

Ideally, I would like to work at a company that is...

If I could describe my best life it would include...

I feel most excited and engaged when I'm...

My greatest sense of accomplishment comes when I...

If I could write my own job description it would include...

My ideal work environment would be...

I want to be most remembered as a great...

Take a moment to really think about your answers. You might want to grab a notebook and do some journaling. Remember these are your honest desires, not what you believe is possible based on past experience. Be truthful with you, and for now don't worry about how your vision will come to fruition.

If you want a job that is remote, say so. If you want a position that is almost solely focused on public speaking, it's out there. Perhaps you want to be a fabulous individual contributor, without ever rising through the ranks to become a senior executive. That is perfectly fine as well. It doesn't make you any less ambitious. You can make an extraordinary impact, leading from any seat.

Listen, we live in a world where playing video games is a viable and often lucrative career. Don't cheat yourself out of what could be by not being honest about what you really want. You deserve the life of your dreams.

In order to get it, however, you're going to have to make some choices and do the work. Let's talk about what you're willing to invest, give up, and prioritize to get what you want.

4. Are you clear about what you're willing to do?

Young women often ask me if can we really have it all. Is it possible to be successful at home and at the office? I always answer with a resounding yes – as long as you define your all, and then determine what you're willing to do to achieve it.

> **Success requires sacrifice. What are you willing to stop doing to start living the life of your dreams?**

Here's a harsh reality – trying to do everything at one time does not produce excellence. It's only through focus that we can deliver our highest and best. That's why if we want to be successful at creating a life and career we love, we've got to make some choices about how, where, and when we show up. This is a critical step in releasing yourself from the pressure of living up or down to unrealistic expectations, many of which have nothing to do with your desired end.

In the previous section we worked to identify your honest desires. Take a stab at summarizing your responses in paragraph form. This will serve as the vision for what you want your life, including your career, to look like. Now let's take a look at what actions best support achieving the state you seek to create.

For your first exercise, let's use a model called "Stop. Start. Continue. Change." (SSCC). Many of you will be familiar with it, as it's been used in business for years for brainstorming, problem solving, and process improvement. Today we're going to use SSCC to decide where to invest your time and energy to move you closer to the life you envision. On the following page is a table to help you think through each step. The questions I've included are to help you craft a plan that is unique for you.

Before you move on to the next chapter you may want to pause and really invest some time here. This is your moment to redirect your mind and actions to creating a life and career you love. You may not be able to answer all of the questions on the following page just yet. That's perfectly natural. What you don't know will become clearer as we go further on our journey. Just make an effort, and then be sure you have a general idea of your strengths, skills, honest desires, and willing to do before going on to lesson two.

Self-awareness is your first step to success and it's the only way to access your space for greatness.

What Are You Willing to Do to Move Toward Your Space for Greatness?	
STOP	What can you stop doing that is not in support of your journey to greatness? Are you committing to too many projects? Is multi-tasking diminishing your excellence? Are you giving too much focus to areas outside of your expertise? Where are you investing your time that is not yielding a return?
START	What can you do to move closer to manifesting your vision? Do you need to build up key skills? Is it time to seek out opportunities that allow you to shine brightest? Do you need to plug into a system that inspires continuous learning? What can you do to support what matters most to you?

CONTINUE	What are you doing now that's right in sync with your space for greatness? Are you in a position that maximizes your strengths? Are your responsibilities in line with your divine design? Have you started investing in your professional development? What area is on the right track and should stay the course?
CHANGE	What's great but could be better? Are you at the right place but in the wrong position? Do you have the right responsibilities but the wrong allocation of time? What small tweak can you make that will yield big dividends?

LESSON TWO

ACTIVATE YOUR UNSTOPPABLE

SUPERPOWER

I'm a huge Marvel super-hero fan. I love characters such as Black Panther, Thor, Iron Man, Doctor Strange, and of course, Black Widow. Some days when I'm feeling less than my best, I wish I had their abilities.

Think of how cool it would be to disappear and rematerialize at your next destination. Wouldn't it be awesome if we could go for hours, and never get tired? I can only imagine all the good we could do if we had our own masks and magic suits.

But then I remember, we don't need any of that. As human beings we are powerful beyond measure. In fact, we are at our strongest when we take off our masks, stop working so hard to be who we think we have to be, and instead, activate our authenticity.

> Authenticity is your unstoppable superpower. There is no one better than you, at being you.

Think about the people you admire for being "authentic." You're likely drawn to them because they consistently provide something you perceive as valuable. You don't worry about how they'll show up or if they'll deliver. You trust them because they have proven to you that they are indeed who they appear to be.

Are they perfect? No, of course not. Like all of us they have weak moments, challenges, and failures. But because they're authentic, they own those moments, make amends, and keep it moving. And because you trust them, you are more likely to extend grace.

Authenticity works because it allows us to create heart to heart connections. Many of us miss out on the joy and freedom of it because it requires two things that can often be quite difficult—vulnerability and intentionality. You see, authenticity is knowing and accepting who you really are, and showing up that way every day. I call it your USP – unstoppable superpower. When you operate in authenticity, your world blossoms with infinite possibilities.

In my first book, *Loving on Me! Lessons Learned on the Journey from Mess to Message*, I talked about how the need to be profound keeps us from activating our authenticity. We're so driven to meet the standards of success, beauty, and significance set by others, that we diminish our own self-worth. Life becomes one big judgement-fest as over and over we find ourselves lacking.

I'm too fat. I'm too skinny.
I'm too dark. I'm too pale.
I'm too old. I'm too young.
I'm under qualified. I'm over qualified.

Whatever the situation, we find a way to tell ourselves I am not enough. The sad thing is, because that's what we believe, it becomes a self-fulfilling prophesy. I see it a lot in the women enrolled in my courses and coaching.

They find a new position that interests them. It's a job they want, but when telling me about it they invariably start in on all the reasons they won't get it. It's as if what they can't do, don't have, or have never done is all they can see.

The interesting thing is, I never ask for any of that information. They volunteer it because they have been conditioned to see themselves through the lens of lack. But I don't allow our conversations to go too far down that road. I have learned that there is no benefit in berating ourselves.

As human beings we respond more positively to affirmation than degradation.

When I'm coaching, I always turn my clients away from the lens of lack, and instead focus their energy on embracing their infinite possibilities.

Just like you and I did in the previous chapter, I help them identify their strengths and unique skill set. We take a look at their track record of success and find examples of their excellence. We discuss how their skills can be applied in other places, and yes, we talk about their areas of challenge, too. The difference is we talk about them not as an area of lack, but of continuous improvement.

My goal is always for them to go forward from a place of authenticity. I want them to see themselves through a clearer, more balanced lens. I know that when they learn to see their value as a human being, and when they appreciate all of the expertise they bring to the table, they can begin to believe that they are enough.

The same can happen for you. Your USP is waiting to be activated. However, in order to do so, you're going to have to turn away from your own lens of lack. In my experience, there are three things that always draws our vision back to our perceived deficiencies—comparing, competing, and complaining. Combined they create a false narrative about our value and worth.

For me, this was an area of challenge long before I joined corporate America. Like many women of color, I was raised to believe that I had to be better than "them" to be successful. To even be in the consideration set for opportunities I had to be more prepared, get better grades, and deliver two to three times more value when given the same investment as my peers. Essentially, I had to be without flaw to flourish in environments where very often I was the only one – be it as a woman or person of color.

This was my truth. I was in a fight to prove my worth, and to claim my seat at the table. My weapon of choice was excellence.

It's an often acknowledged but unspoken reality for people from communities of color. I also find it to be fairly prevalent in many immigrant populations, and with women who work in male-dominated fields. To combat racism and sexism, which are very real barriers to our entry and career elevation, we are taught that we have to be the best.

If you've not had this experience, I imagine that you'll question whether what I'm saying is true. It's difficult to wrap your head around living each day with that kind of pressure. To some degree, I understand your skepticism. After all, if you've never had your differences be seen as deficient, you have no frame of reference for the impact a person's prejudices can have on your life.

It seems ridiculously far-fetched that just because you're a woman, or from a different ethnic group, or don't speak the native tongue as your first language, people would see you as less than, and you'd be given less opportunities. But that's exactly what happens.

The 2018 McKinsey Women in the Workplace[2] study gives a clear picture of the climate in which many of us operate.

✓ For the last three decades women have outpaced men in earning college degrees. Yet, they are less likely to be hired into entry level jobs.

✓ At the first critical step to manager, the disparity widens. For every hundred men promoted, only seventy-nine women advance. Women of color have an even wider gap with only sixty advancing for every one hundred men.

✓ Because of this gender gap, men hold 62% of manager positions, while women hold only 38%. The gap widens with every promotion.

✓ Only about one in five women are senior leaders, and only one in twenty-five is a woman of color.

The struggle for women in the workplace is real, and for women of color, even more so. But so, too, is the opportunity.

Now more than ever there is a substantive focus on gender equity and inclusion. Pay parity is becoming a top priority, too. Recently Starbuck's announced that they had reached 100% pay parity for partners of all genders and races performing similar work across the United States.[3] I believe more companies will soon follow suit.

This is a season ripe with possibilities. We must stay ready, so we don't have to get ready, when opportunity appears.

> Success is when preparation meets opportunity and you recognize it.

So, what does all of this have to do with authenticity? I am so glad you asked! I shared the data on gender equity to give us a clear picture of our circumstances and our psyche.

You see, our propensity to compare, compete, and complain doesn't come out of thin air. For women, there are real issues impacting our ability to access opportunities and excel at the office. However, a part of our challenge is also that we have adopted a mentality of scarcity.

Scarcity convinces you that there are only a few positions available. The statistics tell you that there are less women who will be hired and promoted, so you do whatever you have to do to ensure you're one of them. You're convinced that there are winners and losers, and you don't want to end up on the short end of the stick. As a result, you take what comes along, grabbing whatever is available because, you're afraid of missing out.

When you adopt the mindset of scarcity you place yourself in the position of the victim. Your vision is limited to your circumstances and so, too, are your possibilities. From here you will never be able to live an authentic life. Vulnerability is too risky when you think there is not enough opportunity and everyone is out to best you.

Conversely, let's think about the same circumstances but from the mindset of abundance. In this position you feel empowered. You're convinced that opportunities abound even if they are not currently within your view. Competing with others is not a part of your game plan. Within abundance, there is room for everyone's unique contribution. You're on a personal journey, in search of your unique space for greatness.

With the mindset of abundance, you are in the driver's seat. You look at the challenges before you and get excited about turning them into opportunities. From this space authenticity becomes the key you use to unlock your greatest potential, because your focus is on offering the world your best you, not beating someone else at their own game.

I confess this has been a difficult thing for me to master. Adopting a scarcity mindset was almost second nature, as time and time again, only a few people who look like me were allowed to sit at the table. Sliding into my pattern of being better than "them" was my safe space. It was my comfort zone where I knew that I could shatter their expectations and be viewed as the best. It felt so good to be seen and acknowledged, at least for a moment. But all too soon the feeling would wane and I'd find myself repeating the same cycle, often with the same people.

It took decades of me operating this way before it finally clicked what was wrong with my behavior. You see, I was doing great work, but I wasn't truly satisfied. In fact, many days I felt resentful, because I was constantly trying to prove myself and somebody else was setting the standard.

They were in the driver's seat of my life and I was just along for the ride.

All that comparing, competing, and complaining caused me to focus on "them" and not me. Operating with the mindset of scarcity, believing that there were only a few opportunities, gave me such a narrow vision of my possibilities. I had no idea what it felt like to operate at my highest and best. All I knew was what it felt like to be a little bit better than "them." It's the reason why I could win and still not be satisfied. I was on someone else's journey.

I had to intentionally change my mindset to grow beyond my conditioning and fully embrace my authority over my own life. I also had to mentally move from "them" to us. Opening myself up, even with the possibility of being hurt, was the only way to experience the delight of genuine heart to heart connection. It's also a requirement to lead.

Is it hard? Yes, sometimes it is. I meet people who immediately want to discount me because of the skin I'm in or because of my gender. It triggers me to want to go back to trying to best them. I want to show them I'm smart and worthy. I want to be better than they are so they'll have to respect me and "give me my due." But then, I remember what I have learned.

> I am not competing with you. I am working to be a better me.

This is why I call authenticity our unstoppable superpower. Understanding and embracing who you are, and then choosing to show up as your whole self every day is more powerful than you can imagine. It is the key to your success, peace, and freedom. Authenticity is the highest and best use of your divine design. Anything else, no matter how good it looks, is just a cheap imitation of your greatness.

You deserve the joy of a life without self-imposed limits.

Let's take the blinders off so your mind will allow your eyes to see more of your true self. On the following page is a quick exercise to guide you through your first step of activating your authenticity - defining you. Each thought starter will allow you to look at your life through a different lens.

The key is to keep your focus on you, independent of thinking of how you will measure up to others.

Bear in mind that authenticity is a progression not a destination. When we're hurt, afraid, or triggered by someone else's actions we can easily slide back into our old ways of thinking. The key is to resist the urge to rest there.

Use the allure of pursuing *your* highest and best to draw you closer to your space for greatness. Remind yourself of who you are, regardless of what they say, and then intentionally move forward with confidence in your gifts and grace for your challenges. This is your one life. It is worthy of being lived fully, completely, and abundantly.

The Definition of Me	
I AM	Declaring your "I Am" allows you the great pleasure of defining you. Go beyond your job title and responsibilities into the heart of who you are. A few I use myself are: I am strong. I am worthy. I am a leader. I am creative. I am a beloved child of God. What's your I Am?
I HAVE	Expressing your "I Have" ushers you into a space of gratitude and abundance. It pivots you from looking at yourself through the lens of lack and instead, brings to the forefront all of the assets at your disposal. Here are a few examples to get you thinking. I have health. I have a great education. I have a strong support system. I have a fun personality. What do you have?
I CHOOSE	Embracing your "I Choose" puts you in the driver's seat. It shifts your mind to what you "can do" even when your circumstances aren't ideal. This is where you'll begin to lay out your path forward. You might

	say something like: I choose to face forward, I choose to bring my whole self to work, I choose peace, or I choose to accept myself as I am, and believe that I am enough. What will you choose?

BE BOLD, BE BRILLIANT, BE YOU

LESSON THREE

SIGNAL YOUR SUCCESS READINESS

As a career success strategist, I often connect with people when they've reached a pivot point. Whether it's a desire to move into the ranks of leadership, an interest in exploring new opportunities, or the need to get back on track after a troubling review, their question is often the same. How can I change the perception of me at the office?

My question back is, "What are the signals you're sending to make the impression you want to create?"

We forget that our performance is only one element of what's needed for career success and elevation. Our reputation, co-worker relationships, and readiness to lead are also key drivers. These are three of the many things discussed when making decisions "behind the closed door." That's where leadership meets about you, but doesn't invite you, as they decide what's next for you.

Here's a little secret I want you to keep in mind;

99% of the decisions affecting your career will be made without you in the room.

It happens in many companies as part of an annual staff review where team members are assessed and ranked according to their performance and potential. It can also happen when there's a reorganization, layoff, or expansion. Essentially, it occurs any time leadership needs to make decisions on how best to optimize talent based on available resources.

There are two important things you should know about this process. First, it can happen without any direct feedback from you or given to you. Second, the rankings often determine who is tapped to receive further development or positioned to advance in their career.

It's an uncomfortable truth that many of us struggle to embrace. However, it is bound to happen many times over in your career. Sometimes it's a process that works in our favor. Other times, it leads to incredible frustration, as we seek out ways to be added to the consideration set.

Interestingly, the more favorable outcome happens more often than you think. On the same leadership tour I mentioned in lesson one I asked the attendees, "How many of you are in a position you didn't know was available before leadership contacted you about taking the role?" In each market about 25% of people raised their hands.

Then I asked, "How many of you are in roles that didn't exist before you accepted the role?" Again, another 20- 25% of the people in the room raised their hands. Their response highlights how important it is to prepare and position yourself long before new opportunities emerge.

You see, when leaders go "behind the closed door," they take their observations, conversations, and revelations. Based on those things their perception of you has already been established. So even if you were there, advocating on your own behalf, you'd be fighting against what they already believe to be true about you.

But here's the good news—there is a lot you *can do* to influence their impression of you before they go behind the closed door.

> ## You can have a powerful voice in the room even if you're not present.

To help women accelerate their career success I created the *4 P's of Getting Promoted:* a proven methodology to get noticed, acknowledged, and rewarded for your great work. It teaches you how to send all the right signals so leaders know you are ready to go to the next level.

I love the 4 P's because it puts you in the driver's seat. Step by step it takes you from feeling powerless to empowered, equipping you with the tools you need to successfully navigate your career path.

The graphic on the following page provides a snapshot of the process. The 4 P's is part of my *Career Success Empowerment System™* —a powerful combination of tools and resources to support women leaders create rewarding and fulfilling careers. It's included in one of the many courses leaders can access to boost their confidence and build their competencies in key areas.

It works because of this little secret:

> **Success is formulaic. Our paths are unique. The competencies needed to lead and succeed are consistent.**

Let's take a deep dive into the 4 P's to see what you can do to start sending the right signals to support your success.

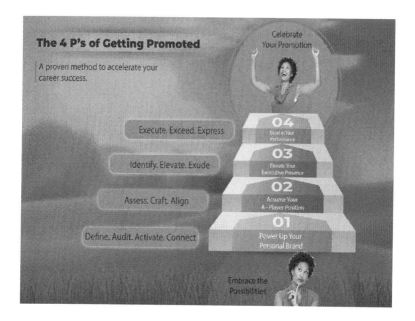

1. Power Up Your Personal Brand

Personal branding is the ongoing process of establishing a prescribed image or impression in the minds of others.[4] There are three key takeaways from that definition that are important.

- ✓ First, it's an "ongoing process." Your personal brand evolves as you do.

- ✓ Second, it's a "prescribed image or impression." You decide how you want to be perceived, and then consciously work to ensure your actions support that impression.

- ✓ Third, if you want to know how you're being perceived, you have to do an audit – courageously asking others for their input.

Just so we're clear, this is not an exercise to make up an alter ego. As we discussed in the previous chapter, authenticity is your unstoppable superpower. It's knowing and accepting who you really are, and then showing up that way every day. The second half of that definition, the consistency of how we show up, is where authenticity intersects with personal branding.

You see, a powerful personal brand is rooted in authenticity. That's where the power comes from. Branding is necessary because it provides a framework for the thoughtful and consistent sharing of your brilliance. It moves us from a reactive, "I'm just going to be me" mentality, to a proactive, "How can I reflect the best in me" intentional response.

Personal branding helps you bring discipline and thought to your actions so they clearly align with your authenticity.

As you think about how to build your personal brand, it's really important to remember that you cannot control other people. Also remember from our discussion on authenticity that we aren't interested in living up or down to someone else's expectations. This is about you defining you, and then choosing to walk your talk at all times. It's also about understanding how people perceive us, and the decisions they are likely to make based on those perceptions.

Remember, behind the closed door are human

beings. They're making decisions about your career based on qualitative and quantitative data, which means observations matter a lot. It is often the lack of clarity about our behavior that causes them to wonder if we're ready to go to the next level.

For example, we present one way in person, then another in our online posts. Or we're positive in some situations, then defensive the next. Sometimes it's that we let circumstances dictate how we react instead of stepping back and deciding how to respond. That, by the way, was my personal struggle in my early 30s.

This is why I'm so passionate about this topic. Being fully present in your choices is a hallmark of a great leader. I had to learn it, and you can, too. When you master the 4 P's you'll send all the right signals about your temperament and character.

Following is a checklist of things you can do in the next thirty days to power up your personal brand. It's an action plan to ensure you show up in a way that is both clear and captivating.

✓ Define your brand, clearly articulating who you are and how you want to show up. (Hint: use the work you've done in lesson one and two to get you started.)

✓ Identify ways to share your knowledge and expertise. Whether you curate or create content, become a trusted resource for valuable insights and information.

✓ Dress for your position and ambition. Make sure your outer appearance reflects your inner brilliance.

✓ Develop your own social media guidelines governing what you will post, and when. Be sure to share it with friends and remove any posts that are out of alignment.

✓ Confirm your LinkedIn profile is complete. Your online presence should accurately reflect your expertise.

2. Assume Your A-Player Position

Everyone can be an A-Player. However some of us

are out of position. It can happen for a whole host of reasons. Perhaps the job you were hired to do, the one aligned with your space for greatness, is no longer your role. It could also be that you've had to take on additional responsibilities because of team reorganizations or departures. Whatever the reasons, when our core responsibilities are not in sync with our strengths and skills, we struggle to excel.

This can be a source of infinite frustration or an opportunity to explore some new alternatives.

Now, if you completely dislike your job, the answer is simple – you need a new one. You should not work hard at a job you hate, and you'll never do your best at something you don't enjoy. It's time to take the work you did in lesson one and go look for a new role.

However, if you like your job or the place where you work, but still feel like you're underutilizing your expertise, we need a different strategy. Let's run through a series of questions to try and identify the best solution for getting you back in alignment.

Are your strengths, skills, and desires clear?

In lesson one we talked about the importance of understanding your expertise and desires as a means of identifying your space for greatness. Before you embark on any strategy to change positions, be sure you're clear about your expertise, how you use it to bring value to the organization, and what your life priorities are in this season.

Sometimes it's not the job responsibilities that are the issue. It's how you want to live your life that is out of alignment with your position. Taking a moment here to get to the root of the issue will ensure you select the right strategy to course correct.

Is the cause of your discontent temporary?

Often there are short-term changes that cause periods of increased work load and shuffling of responsibilities. This could be because of staff departures, budget freezes, or delays in deployment of other assets. If this is the case, even if it's for a full fiscal year, you may want to stick it out. Showing flexibility, adaptability, and poise under pressure are all great ways to signal that you are ready to lead and succeed.

Are you willing to learn the required skills?

Sometimes positions feel like they're outside of our space for greatness when they're actually outside of our comfort zone. The work we've been assigned to do is still aligned with our strength. However, it requires some skill building on our part to excel.

This scenario requires some honest introspection on your part. There are certainly benefits to learning new skills that align with your strengths. Increasing your marketability, developing a broader base of knowledge, and staying current on industry trends and new technology are a few.

But if you know that you have no interest in learning what's required, it's time to look for new a role that allows you to be an asset to the organization. Staying in a role where you're discontent and not growing is bad business for you and for the organization.

Does leadership support your success?

This is the most critical component necessary to allow you to stay with your company, and still get back into alignment with your space for greatness. If there are leaders within the organization that support your success, you can almost always find a solution. It likely won't be overnight but with patience, planning, and flexibility, it is achievable. Here's how I recommend you go forward:

- ✓ Deliver the highest value you can within your current role. Even outside your space for greatness you can still make a difference.

- ✓ Prepare to have a logical, fact-based, conversation that outlines your concerns and offers viable solutions. It's very important that you don't go in with an emotional complaint that doesn't take into account the current needs of the company and the value you bring. Your goal is to identify a win-win strategy.

- ✓ Schedule a meeting with the leader who can be most supportive in further refining your solution or moving toward a decision. This may be your direct supervisor, or you may want to talk it over with an internal mentor or champion.

- ✓ Finally, make sure you approach the whole process with a mindset of abundance and a spirit of can-do. Bringing a positive attitude to the discussion often makes a world of difference in how your suggestions are received.

Even when you do everything right, there are going to be times when the organization's needs change. There may not be a role that aligns with your areas of expertise. It is okay. Things happen, and we have to adapt. Embrace abundance and go forth believing there is a space for your greatness to shine bright.

3. Elevate Your Executive Presence

Executive presence is one of those elusive areas that's hard to define, but you know it when you see it. When people with executive presence walk in, they are often described as "owning the room." They exude authority even when they aren't in charge.

They also exhibit excellent communication skills and a high level of discernment, reading and understanding non-verbal cues that provide a richer context for discussions.

It's a requirement for any senior leader – with employers indicating up to 26% of their decisions on who to promote being dependent on the candidate's ability to embody it.[5] But who exhibits executive presence, and to what degree, is highly subjective.

An easy way to think about it is to remember that executive presence is comprised of three things: style, substance, and character. For leadership, it essentially answers this question:

Am I assured that you will comport yourself appropriately, with confidence and authority, in a room full of senior executives?

If you've been encouraged to work on this, well, first let me say, good for you, and kudos to whomever gave you the feedback. Often this is an area supervisors don't know how to address because they're basing their opinion on general observations—or feedback that has come from above—and they can't figure out how to give you practical advice to improve in this area.

Instead, they talk to you about speaking up and taking the initiative. They may also challenge you to better communicate your ideas or work on your confidence. All of these are important, but just saying them doesn't really give you actionable steps you can take for improvement.

Let's take a look at the five dimensions of executive presence on the following page to see if you can identify any of your specific areas of challenge. Once you have a sense of where you may be struggling, we'll dive into strategies for your success. Grab your notebook so you can jot down a few notes as you answer the questions on the chart.

———————————

Reading this list of traits, it can seem a bit daunting to become this paragon of professionalism. But I want you to remember that no one came out of their momma's womb with confidence, gravitas, and poise under pressure. These are all learned behaviors.

With awareness, practice, and consistency, it's possible for you to improve in every area. Let's look at how we can help you stand out in a way that sets you up for success. Below are strategies for elevating your presence in each of the areas above.

5 Dimensions of Executive Presence	
ATTITUDE	- Do you have a positive attitude at the office? - Are you embracing a can-do spirit? - Do you stay cool, even under pressure?
APPEARANCE	- Is your attire reflective of your position and ambition? - Do you practice good posture? - Are you polished in your presentation even on casual day?
ARTICULATION	- Are you confident in your communication? - Do you use an engaging voice and tone when speaking? - Is your messaging clear and succinct or are you rambling?
AMBITION	- Do you take strategic risks or refuse to leave your safe zone? - Are you a solution seeker or merely a problem presenter? - Do you seek out areas where you can give value based on your expertise?

ACTION	- Do you take the initiative or wait to be asked to complete a task? - Do you procrastinate or activate? - Are you decisive and dedicated to moving projects forward? - Do you follow-up and follow through?

Attitude

If attitude is your challenge, I recommend three activities to help keep you in the right frame of mind.

First, set the tone for your day. Before your feet hit the floor express a moment of gratitude. Put yourself in a mindset of abundance by focusing on all you have and have accomplished.

Second, schedule yourself joy breaks at least once a day. This is fifteen minutes where you allow yourself to be present and enjoy the moment. Sometimes I go for a walk outside and soak up some vitamin D. Other days I make myself a peppermint mocha, or just sit and focus on my breathing. Choose what soothes you. You'll be amazed what it does for your balance and peace of mind.

Finally, I recommend everyone have a song, a saying, and a dance.

> **You are your own best cheerleader and worst critic. It all depends on what you choose to say to yourself.**

When I need to shake off the blues or give myself a boost of energy, I pop on Michael Jackson. His music always gets me energized and moving. I also have different mantras I say to myself to focus my energy in the right direction. Some of your "I Am" statements from the previous chapter may be good for helping you reframe the narrative running in your head.

Appearance

This is such an uncomfortable area to discuss. As leaders it's challenging to address it head on because it's so subjective, and it can be pretty hard to hear. Let me just cut to the chase and say it to you straight. We cannot come to work dressed a hot mess. I know some of you feel that what you wear shouldn't be important. You believe the focus should be on your excellent performance, not on whether you meet a standard of professional dress set by someone else.

Well, I completely agree that the focus should be on your performance. That's why we have to ensure that your style is distinct, not a distraction. In a 2012 Center for Talent Innovation study of senior leaders, 83% said unkept attire detracts from a woman's executive presence; 73% said too-tight or provocative clothing also diminishes a woman's presence.[6] It may seem unfair, but appearance matters.

In a world that is becoming increasingly casual, to dress with care is a wonderful way to stand out and position yourself as success ready. You have two goals when deciding what to wear: first, make sure your inner brilliance is reflected in your outer appearance, and second, make sure your outer appearance isn't a distraction from your excellent performance.

On my YouTube channel "IAmLovingonMe" there is a "Dress for Success" video highlighting areas we often overlook. Watch it to see if any of the tips resonate with you. If you really struggle in this area, proactively seek out a stylist. Most department stores have them, and they're a great resource in helping you pick out the colors, style, and size that best compliment you.

Articulation

In the next chapter we're going to focus on communication so let's chat here about the sound and cadence of your voice. Have you ever listened to a recording of yourself presenting or leading a meeting? What's the energy of your voice? Is it flat and monotone, or does it have variation and enthusiasm? Do you talk really fast or do you communicate with a slower rhythm?

When it comes to executive presence, the goal is to project confidence when we communicate. To do so, we have to work with the natural rhythm of our voice to exude energy and enthusiasm. It's possible with either a fast or slow cadence, as long as we're conscious of using variation in our tone.

The best way to get better is to be clear about how you sound, and then consciously work to add the variation. It's important because it allows the listener to connect to your content and your emotion. It's amazing how much more engaged people are when they can tell you're passionate about your subject. Your enthusiasm, and belief in the words you're saying encourages them to buy in, too.

If you find yourself constantly communicating in a flat tone, here is what I recommend. Purchase a children's book with multiple characters. Challenge yourself to come up with a different voice for each character, and then read the book out loud, as if you were bringing the story to life for a child.

Record yourself. Listen to the variations in your tone. Become intimately familiar with how you sound when you're infusing your voice with emotion. This will give you a sense of what's possible when you intentionally choose to share your passion with others.

Then I want you to incorporate using similar variations as you practice your presentations. The more you work at it the easier it will become. If you want to accelerate your progress ask a colleague to be your accountability partner. They can serve as your practice buddy and give you real-time feedback after presentations and meetings.

Ambition

The biggest deterrent to our taking strategic risks is our fear of failure. We don't want to put our ideas out there because they might be wrong or perceived as half-baked. It feels like the safe thing to do is stay in our lane, where we know we can knock it out of the park.

The problem with that approach is twofold. First, if you're not stretching yourself beyond your comfort zone you're not growing. **Leaders master learning.** If we want to accelerate our careers, we have to be willing to try and fail.

To keep you encouraged write the words below on a sticky and post it somewhere prominent. If you have a team, you may want to share it with them, too.

Success and failure are events, never people.

When you learn to see failure as a natural part of your journey, especially when you're growing and learning new skills, it will greatly diminish your fear of the experience.

The second challenge with staying in the safe zone is that you miss out on teachable moments. Most leaders would love that you proactively think of solutions for problems you bring to their attention. Even if you can't completely solve the problem, they can see your approach, and help you make adjustments to get to a solution.

This increases your knowledge and helps you become a better problem solver. It also impresses leadership because it shows that you are solution-oriented and willing to take initiative. It's a win-win on multiple levels.

Action

One of the surest ways for leadership to lose confidence in us is when we don't follow through and finish strong. We're great starters, but far less of us are committed to closure. When things get busy, we start trying to do everything at one time. We multi-task in hopes that we can do more in less time and not get behind.

It sounds reasonable, but it's actually contrary to all the research. According to a recent study the human brain was not designed to focus on more than one task at a time. Multi-tasking kills brain cells, reduces mental acumen, and reduces productivity.[7]

Multi-tasking is the kryptonite of productivity.

Yikes! I don't know about you but I can't afford to lose any brain cells from trying to do too much at one time. Nor do we have to when there is a better way. Rather than trying to do everything at once, which greatly diminishes our ability to deliver excellence, let's focus on finishing strong.

This is your best strategy for keeping your sanity and staying true to your commitment to excellence. Listen, I know you have a lot of responsibilities. It's almost laughable to think we can lay everything else down and do just one thing. The key is to prioritize and bring all of our brain power to the most important activity, for that moment. It takes discipline, but it's doable.

It's the best way for you to rock the last of the 4 P's, excelling in your performance.

4. Excel in Your Performance

The first three steps focused on preparing and positioning you to stand out in a way that sets you up for success. However, in order to go to the next level or be granted some of the flexibility and freedom you're seeking, you have to consistently deliver on this last step, excelling in your performance.

Here's a little insight for some of you who

consistently meet your goals but are never considered for promotion.

> Meeting your goals is the bare minimum. That keeps you employed. Getting promoted requires exceeding your goals. This clearly signals to leadership that you are ready for more responsibility.

This is unpopular, I know. We want to believe that when we meet the goals our boss set for us, we will be rewarded with more. But most senior leaders will tell you that in some way they were already doing elements of the job they were promoted into, or at a minimum exhibiting the skills needed to successfully transition, before they were promoted into a bigger role. It was their internal standard of excellence, going beyond their goals, that propelled them to higher ground.

Now, I'm sure some of you are thinking of exceptions to what I just said. Are there people who consistently deliver mediocrity and still manage to get promoted? Yes, absolutely. When a person like that is selected over you for an opportunity, or worse, you have to report to them, that is a signal to you that it's time for an assessment.

Listen if you're operating in a dysfunctional environment where nepotism, sexism, ageism, or favoritism are the norm, these principles will not fix it. This book is about putting you in the driver's seat of your life, so you can create the career path you desire. So, if you're facing circumstances where unfair or unreasonable practices are taking place, go back to the section on "Getting in Position" to decide if you're in the best place for you.

If you want to stay, get some counsel from a good coach or attorney that knows employment law for your state on what recourse you might have to fight the discrimination you perceive you're facing. Make sure you also ask for candid feedback, and then consider whether it resonates with your spirit.

Sometimes there are areas that are distracting from our performance, such as the things we discussed in personal branding and executive presence. Attitudes and actions that may be no big deal to us could be having a profound impact on the impression leaders are taking behind the closed door. Whether you agree with the feedback or not, it's always good to know what's being said about you. This arms you with the data you need to make an informed choice that's in your best interest.

If you do decide you want to explore other options, use what we discussed in lesson one and the positioning section to guide you. You want to give your all at a place where you believe you can be your best.

Excellence is a way to positively differentiate you, exhibiting abilities that go far beyond the status quo. It's not just about reaching the goal, it's about how you did it, and who you brought along for the journey. It's a habit, and done consistently, can have a profound impact on the path of your career.

We've covered a lot of ground in this chapter. I want you to take a moment to reflect on what resonated with you. On the following page is a chart for you to complete. Outline what you'll do in the next thirty days to put the *4 P's of Getting Promoted* to work for you.

My 4 P's of Getting Promoted Action Plan

Make a commitment to you to get prepared and positioned to lead and succeed.

To Power Up My Personal Brand I Will:

1. _____
2. _____
3. _____

To Get In A-Player Position I Will:

4. _____
5. _____
6. _____

To Elevate My Executive Presence, I Will:

7. _____
8. _____
9. _____

To Excel in My Performance I Will:

10. _____

11. _____

12. _____

LESSON FOUR

COMMUNICATE YOUR BRILLIANCE

WITH CONFIDENCE

———————

Of all the competencies I help career executives master, those related to communicating are some of the hardest. Presentation skills are especially difficult because of their public nature. Eight percent of women and 6% of men in America have a fear of public speaking.[8] Based on my anecdotal research from teaching and mentoring I'd guess a strong dislike is held by millions more.

I'm always fascinated by the reasons even seasoned professionals give for their aversion. The one response that always makes me laugh is when someone says, "I don't like everyone looking at me." Wait, what? Let me see if I've got this right. You want to be a people leader, but you don't want people to actually see you? Oh, okay, you want to be invisible while doing it.

We always get a chuckle out of that, because when I say it out loud, it's clear that won't fly. If you want to lead and succeed you have to be able to communicate your brilliance with confidence. It's both essential and exponential.

Warren Buffet said, "You can improve your value by 50% just by learning communication skills—public speaking.[9]" He was talking to a group of college students who were just about the same age he was when he enrolled in a class to conquer his own fear of public speaking. It took him signing up twice before he graduated from the course. Years later, he still proudly displays his certificate.

I love his story because it's an awesome reminder that no matter how great our fears, we can be better. If communicating with confidence is difficult for you, don't be discouraged. There are courses, tools and resources to help you overcome it.

In this chapter I want to provide you with a framework I've created to help you conquer one of the more common challenges. I call it the "virus of rambling." Nearly everyone I meet has it, and as yet I have found no permanent cure.

The symptoms can lay dormant for long periods of time, but then unexpectedly manifest in an alarming fashion when we're stressed, excited, exhausted, anxious, or unprepared.

You know you're suffering a flair up of the virus when you begin to experience an uncontrollable vomiting of words. You can't seem to stop yourself, as barely coherent phrases continually spill from your mouth, with no apparent end. You know there was a reason you started speaking, but soon it's lost on you and the listener, as you both struggle to make sense of your garbled message.

There's a video entitled "Communication Gone Wrong" on my YouTube channel. Check it out to see if this sounds like someone you know.

When you're on a rambling rampage you feel out of control. Your only recourse to end the madness is to stop talking and pray desperately that your mind soon catches up with your mouth. Most all of us have had this experience a time or two – either as the speaker or the listener. When rambling begins the ability to effectively communicate ends.

> **Effective communication is a shared conversation with messaging that is clear, concise, and complete, delivered in context, consistently.**

Rambling is particularly obstructive when communicating with senior leadership. Their time constraints, coupled with the more direct communication style most prefer, makes it difficult to come back from a bout of rambling. It's likely that you'll be sent away and not summoned again for quite a long time. Eventually it becomes a challenge to share your ideas when you can't even get an audience.

I confess I'm one of those leaders that cannot abide rambling. It drives me nuts. I have a lion personality, so when it has to do with business, I like people to get to the point. I don't want to know how the clock works. I just want to know what time it is. If I have questions after you topline it, I'll ask.

Because I know that's how my personality is most likely to react, I've worked hard to discipline myself to respond with patience. Instead of just shutting people down I try to coach them on how to be better communicators. It's been so much fun to watch people make huge leaps in their communication competency as they become more confident in their delivery.

But in full transparency I have to tell you this is an approach I adopted much later in my career. In particular, my days as a director were full and in many cases overflowing, especially when you factored in my travel. Those middle management positions where you are still doing so much of the work, while also trying to be a good leader, don't leave a lot of room for personalized coaching. It can be a bit frustrating on both sides.

That's why I want to lay out a framework here to help you get organized. On the following page are six steps that will guide you in crafting a message that is clear, concise and complete. It will also help you think through the context in which you're delivering your message, and because you've planned it out, you'll stay consistent.

Use this framework to develop a presentation, craft

an email, or lay out an agenda for an in-person meeting. It follows a logical pattern that allows the listener to join the conversation happening in your head. It also gives you natural pauses so that you don't rush through, as we often do when we're nervous.

It may seem overly simplified, but that's intentional. Albert Einstein said, "The definition of genius is taking the complex and making it simple." I've made these steps as basic as possible so people at every level can understand and adopt them. I've also crafted it this way as an example

6 Steps to Communicate Any Idea
with Confidence

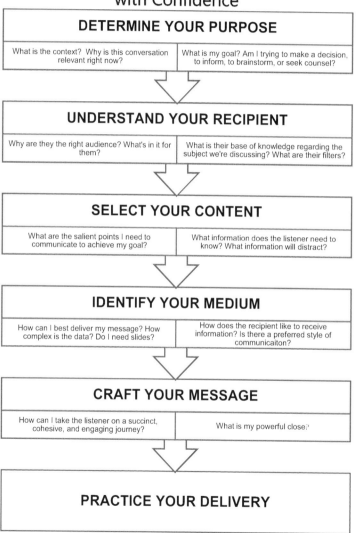

DETERMINE YOUR PURPOSE

| What is the context? Why is this conversation relevant right now? | What is my goal? Am I trying to make a decision, to inform, to brainstorm, or seek counsel? |

UNDERSTAND YOUR RECIPIENT

| Why are they the right audience? What's in it for them? | What is their base of knowledge regarding the subject we're discussing? What are their filters? |

SELECT YOUR CONTENT

| What are the salient points I need to communicate to achieve my goal? | What information does the listener need to know? What information will distract? |

IDENTIFY YOUR MEDIUM

| How can I best deliver my message? How complex is the data? Do I need slides? | How does the recipient like to receive information? Is there a preferred style of communicaiton? |

CRAFT YOUR MESSAGE

| How can I take the listener on a succinct, cohesive, and engaging journey? | What is my powerful close? |

PRACTICE YOUR DELIVERY

for you to follow when you are communicating more involved concepts.

When you're in a business setting, resist the urge to be impressive and instead, aim for relatable and relevant. Remember, effective communication requires active listening and response. Overly complex slides and graphics with lots of words and symbols often distract from clarity. They also reduce the effectiveness of your message.

Make your top priority a shared understanding of the data so that you can achieve your established goal for communicating. Trust me, if you do that, you'll be impressive.

Before we close out this chapter let me briefly touch on two more topics: improving your presentation skills and the proper way to practice.

First, if you know that presenting is a challenge for you, I recommend that you hire a communications coach, find an in-person course, or join an organization such as Toastmasters. You need to plug into a system that teaches you everything from the proper way to create and utilize slides, to how to stand so that the energy flows freely through your body. Otherwise you could find yourself fainting.

When I teach my *Presenting with Power* course it's always in person and includes individualized feedback. I love my online Academy, and for many subjects – like the 4 P's, it's an amazing experience. But teaching people how to present is something I have learned is best delivered face-to-face.

Is it more nerve-wracking for you? Sure! You're getting real-time feedback. But on the flip side, it's teaching based on your unique style and cadence. If you really want to master presenting, find a course you can attend that offers one-on-one work with an instructor.

Now, when it comes to practice, whether you're a novice or a seasoned presenter, you've got to go beyond just running through your talk in your head. Here are a few strategies to maximize your prep time.

✓ To make sure you start with a cohesive and succinct narrative I recommend writing out your talk track with a pen and paper. You're not going to take this with you when you present. It's purely to organize your thoughts and to increase your comprehension. Studies have shown that people who write things out longhand versus typing the information process it on a deeper level.[10] That's why throughout this course I've challenged you to grab a notebook and spend time reflecting.

✓ Once you're satisfied with your talk track, convert it to typed bullet points. This is what you want to utilize when you actually give your presentation. Using the longhand version of your notes will flatten the tone of your voice as you are more likely to read your story. It's also sometimes hard to keep your place when your information is in paragraph form. If you can't completely go with bullet points be sure to double space your paragraphs.

✓ Using your bullet points, record yourself giving your talk. Be sure you stand while giving the presentation. Even if you're at home you want to mimic being on your feet. Your voice and energy are different when you stand versus when you sit.

✓ During your dry run, familiarize yourself with any electronic devices you'll use during your presentation. This is especially important if it's not the computer you use every day, or you'll be connecting into projection or audio devices. I don't care how many times you've used it, it's good to run through it before your presentation.

✓ When you're done recording, play it back, but only listen to the audio. This will allow you to assess your message content, structure and close without being distracted by seeing yourself on the screen. Also pay close attention to your tone and when you use filler words such as "uh," "and," "really," and "like." They can be very distracting so you may need to work on the talk track in those areas.

✓ Then I want you to play the recording a second time and watch the presentation. This time focus on your delivery. Look for unconscious mannerisms and gestures that may distract the listener. Also watch your facial expression. This is important even if you're going to be presenting from a remote location and people won't be able to see you. Smiles, frowns, confusion, and enthusiasm can be heard in your voice. Make sure you're expressing them at the proper time.

✓ Your next round of practice should be in front of a small group. It helps to practice by yourself but at some point, you need to mimic the nervousness you'll feel when presenting prior to the presentation. This will allow you to notice your body's natural reaction. For example, if you sweat excessively, you'll want to select your clothes with that in mind when you present.

✓ Finally, ask for feedback from your small group. Doing this well in advance of your actual presentation will allow you to make tweaks and practice again. Don't wait until the last minute to try and get a group together. It will increase your nervousness, versus put your mind at ease.

Proper practice makes for a powerful presentation. Invest the time to ensure you show up prepared and confident. It will reduce the likelihood of you rambling, increase your impact on your audience, and allow your brilliance to shine through.

BE BOLD, BE BRILLIANT, BE YOU

LESSON FIVE

CULTIVATE YOUR CAN-DO

CONNECTIONS

———————

Understanding your strengths and areas of challenge allows you to offer your best with confidence. When coupled with strong communication skills, powerful executive presence, and excellence in your performance, you send all the right signals that you're ready to lead and succeed. These all work together to put you in the driver's seat. But it's only when you cultivate your can-do connections that you can put the car in gear and accelerate your career.

This is an often under nourished yet essential

component of our success. You see, our can-do connections are people who help us get things done. More than just a "network" of people we know, these are deeper relationships with supporters who provide perspective, power our progress, and open up pathways to reach our goals.

Cultivating these connections is super important, and yet the majority of professional women I meet struggle in this area. We let online networks do the work for us, clicking the "connect" tab as a way of checking "building connections" off our list. It allows us to sit behind our computer screen and engage superficially by liking posts and sending a note of congrats for promotions. It's a great first step to at least stay in touch with people you respect and admire. But you can't confuse online networking with the can-do connections that pay dividends in your career.

Those require a bit more effort and intention. They also require time, something most of us have in short supply. In the midst of busy lives, spending time with people outside of close friends and family, no matter how helpful to our career, often becomes less of a priority. Even the thought of it can be overwhelming.

Trust me, I understand. The majority of my career I was a single parent. I had very little time for happy hours, networking events, or many of the other out of the office functions that would allow me to get to know other professionals, let alone build connections. But at the same time, I knew that I needed the support of a myriad of other people to succeed.

This became clear to me when I first started at the oil and gas company I told you about. Hired as part of a class of twenty or so new recruits, we were each assigned an individual trainer to show us the ropes. They also regularly brought us together for group onboarding activities and networking. It was an awesome way to start my professional career.

My trainer was an African-American woman who had been with the organization for some time. Given that back then oil and gas was a male-dominated field, and there were very few women rising through the ranks, it was really a gift to be able to learn from her. She schooled me on not only how to do the job, but also on the benefits of building alliances with my colleagues.

She also challenged me to get involved in industry organizations, such as the National Association of Black

Accountants. She stressed the importance of intentionally connecting with people who had been where I was going and could help me navigate the waters. So, with what little out of the office time I had, I invested in the relationships that would yield the greatest return in my life.

That's what I want to help you do, too.

There are five can-do connections every professional woman needs to cultivate to create a rewarding and fulfilling career. Check them out to see if you're well connected, or you've got some work to do.

The Mentor

The most impactful relationships on my career and my business have been with my mentors. They are the people I've looked to time and time again to help me put things in perspective, and to help me problem-solve when I'm at my wit's end. Every successful person I know or have read about, has had at least one mentor, and many have more than one at the same time.

If you're considering whether or not you need one, the answer is yes. There is not a person I know who won't benefit from the wisdom of someone a little further down the path. The question is where do you find one?

Mentors can come from within or outside of your organization. Ideally, you'd have both. That way when things are tense at the office you can get perspective from a person that's not emotionally engaged with the issue. As a general rule, there are three ways to connect with a mentor: organically, organizationally, or proactively.

Most of my mentor relationships have happened organically. They developed as a result of meeting people with whom I had a genuine interest. There was something I admired about them, or vice versa, and we made an effort to get to know each other. I asked about their life, followed their work, took their courses, and actively sought out ways to get to know them. As a result, they got to know me, too. It's amazing how great relationships can develop from curiosity and respect.

I also know many people who have been assigned a mentor. Like the relationship I described with my trainer, their company pairs young professionals with more seasoned executives to support their growth and development. In this case to fully benefit from the experience it's imperative that you invest the time to get to know your mentor. It's also important that you be open to be a part of things in which they find value. The more receptive you are, the more they'll share their resources, connections, and expertise.

Be sure to share enough of yourself that they get to know you, too. Remember, mentors give you perspective. They need a good sense of your values, lifestyle and goals to offer advice in context. It's also a good idea to look for ways you can add value to their life, as building a strong connection takes work on both sides.

If you haven't been assigned a mentor, or you don't meet one organically, seek one out proactively. Just be sure to keep this in mind;

Mentorship is rooted in relationship.

It's usually not effective to walk up to someone you admire, but don't really know and ask them to be your mentor. Busy people tend to avoid those that are presumptive about their time. Taking a more measured approach generally yields better results.

Here are four questions to help you get a clear picture of the mentor that will be a good match for you.

✓ What are the key areas in which I'm seeking improvement?

✓ Would I prefer someone within or outside of my organization?

✓ Do I want consistent interaction or an occasional check-in?

✓ What personality type best aligns with my own?

Once you know what you need, you now have to put yourself in spaces where you are likely to meet potential mentors. Internally that may mean volunteer opportunities, mixers, or cross-functional projects. Externally it's often conferences, courses, and professional organizations such as the one my trainer suggested for me.

This will introduce you to a pool of people with whom you may have common interests and experiences. When you identify someone you respect and admire, invest time in getting to know them. Take their courses and participate in giving feedback. Read their books and listen to their public lectures. Follow and engage with them on social media.

Take some time to observe their interests, temperament, and expertise.

> **Express genuine interest to get the attention of those you admire most. Intentionally put yourself in their orbit and explore what they have to offer.**

Also, think about what you can give that adds value to their life. Your aim is a mutually beneficial relationship that enriches you both.

When you approach them about being your mentor, be sure to share what you respect about their work or expertise. This will give them context why you've selected them. Then specifically ask for what you want: help reaching a goal, developing a skill, or improving your performance in a key area.

Being explicit about what you need gives the potential mentor options. Ideally, they'll be receptive to your request and readily say yes. However, this is not always the case. For a whole host of reasons, that in some cases have nothing to do with you, they may decline.

The good news is when they know what you need even when they can't mentor you, they may help you identify someone who can. The key is to be open to alternatives so you don't miss out on a great opportunity.

The Sponsor

When mentors offer their perspective, it helps you improve your performance and positioning. This is often what sets you apart and *attracts* a sponsor, one of the single most influential people in the trajectory of your career. They are the power brokers with the influence and authority to open up new pathways in your career.

Sponsors are influential leaders that position and promote other leaders. They're not just identifying A-players. They are leveraging their credibility to strategically move them from one position to the next, advancing business objectives and accelerating careers.

One of the pivotal roles many sponsors play is to help more women access leadership positions. As we discussed in lesson two, while women get more college degrees, as they advance in their career they are represented less and less in executive roles. Sponsors in many industries are working to change that, so that more women are coached for and promoted into leadership positions.

The question is how do you secure a sponsor?

Well, this is a bit tricky. Some experts recommend that you attract, don't ask for a sponsor. Others think you shouldn't sit around just waiting for someone to notice you. They recommend identifying an influential leader within the organization who knows your work and approaching them with a request for sponsorship.

As a person who has been sponsored, and sponsored others, I tend to go with the first approach. However, I recognize in very large multi-layered organizations you may need to be more proactive. Either way, my recommendation is to begin your quest for a sponsor by fully implementing the *4 P's of Getting Promoted.*

Sponsors align themselves with stellar performers with stand-out reputations. When you connect with one, there is an expectation that you will stand and deliver. Very often they'll ask you to go above and beyond, serving on cross-functional committees, or in volunteer leader roles. This is so they can position you to be seen and considered for advancement by other leaders.

It should be noted that your supervisor is very often not your sponsor. It's not that they don't want to see you grow. Your supervisor simply may not have enough influence or authority to advance your career. They can, however, play a pivotal role in recruiting other leaders to speak up on your behalf. That's why it's good to ensure you have great relationships with everyone in the leadership pipeline.

Sponsors often come from two or more levels above you, and many times are from different areas of the organization. Your relationship with them will be very different than the one with your mentor or boss. Many women make the mistake of looking for sponsors they "like." Similar to their mentor, they're looking for someone with the same temperament as their own. However, when it comes to your sponsor this has no bearing.

A sponsor's focus is not to mentor or coach you. They may do some of that as they position you for promotion, but their primary role in your life is to unlock new opportunities for your career. Don't let differences in leadership style or personality discourage you from connecting with leaders who can support your success. If you want a sponsor be flexible and stay ready.

The Coach

Another key relationship that we often overlook is with a coach. Over the years I've had a number of them, and one of my favorites described our work together by saying, "I'll shine the light. You do the work." I remember it because it described beautifully what good coaches do – lead you through a process of discovery.

The best coaches ask insightful questions that help illuminate your path forward. Step by step, they help you find solutions that take you ever closer to your goals. They don't do the work for you, but they can minimize your anxiety as you get it done.

At the office, coaching sometimes gets a bad rap because it's presented as an "opportunity" during a challenging end of year review. When leadership notices us struggling in a key area they often recommend or require we spend time with an executive coach. It can seem like punishment for poor performance. You may even feel a bit embarrassed to need the help.

But when viewed from a more positive perspective coaching can be transformational. A good coach can equip you with the tools you need to change your life. Moreover, they teach you how to think about things differently, so that when you're faced with challenges in the future you are better able to respond with confidence.

I love coaches. If you're struggling in a specific area, I recommend that you hire one for yourself. These days there are coaches for a variety of different focus areas, some certified and others who are not. Having met hundreds of practitioners, what I can tell you for certain is that there are excellent certified coaches, and there are those who don't pursue an official certification but are incredibly experienced and impactful. Their credentials are only one thing to consider when selecting the person that's right for you.

Here are a few additional questions to ask yourself so you can connect with your best coach.

✓ Why do I want to see a coach? What is my area of need?

- ✓ What am I hoping to achieve? How will I measure success?

- ✓ Is there a specific expertise my coach must possess?

- ✓ Am I looking for a person who works with professionals at a certain level?

- ✓ How do I want to engage with my coach: in person, Skype, email, or over the phone?

- ✓ What is my budget—in terms of time and money?

When you have a sense of what you need and who you're looking for, I suggest asking your trusted advisers for recommendations. There's nothing like positive "word-of-mouth" feedback from people you believe have great judgement and insight. Mentors, human resource professionals, and colleagues who have had coaches are a great place to start.

If your budget is tight, take a look at group coaching options. This is often more economical and has the added bonus of giving you a community of like-minded people. I've added it to our career success system and it's made a world of difference. An environment of shared learning allows women to learn from each other, often providing fresh approaches to address their challenges.

Whichever option you choose I encourage you to have fun. A coaching relationship requires work, but it shouldn't be drudgery. Enjoy your journey of self-discovery.

The Collaborator

The first three relationships focused on preparing and positioning you to accelerate your career. The collaborator, however, has your back in getting the job done. This is the person who helps you excel in your performance even when it's not their responsibility to do so.

I'm talking about colleagues and friends who will stay late, come in on the weekends, and help you figure out challenges on your desk that have nothing to do with their own. They assist you for no other reason than the connection you two share. Their delight is seeing you succeed, and they need nothing from you but gratitude.

I thought it important to include people like this for two reasons. First, sometimes we fall into the "pulling ourselves up by our own boot strap" mentality. We get to thinking we can do it all on our own, when in truth no one can achieve greatness without selfless people who support our goals. In fact, we're not supposed to.

Human beings are creatures of interconnectedness. We're designed to support each other, each bringing unique strengths and abilities to every task. It may sound a bit trite but it really is true—we are stronger together.

> When we effectively collaborate, we become force multipliers, dramatically increasing productivity and possibility.

To get people to go above and beyond in the way I've described above, we must be willing to do so ourselves. As you look for people to get in the trenches with you, ask yourself, "Who am I willing to collaborate with?" If you can't think of anyone then you probably don't have anyone.

Collaboration that goes beyond what colleagues are expected to do, requires getting to know people and allowing them to know you beyond your professional mask. I know that's a scary proposition. As we discussed in lesson two, vulnerability opens you up to being hurt as well as building beautiful connections.

Sometimes you have no idea which way it's going to go, but when your intuition tells you to get to know someone, take a strategic risk. Open up and make space for others to do the same. Heart to heart connections are soothing for the soul and show up to support your success in ways you would not even imagine.

The second reason I included collaborators was because I wanted to encourage you to stop and say thanks. When you express gratefulness, you complete the karmic exchange that begins when someone shows you kindness. It allows both you and your collaborator to feel worthy and rewarded for your efforts. Don't let the little things that mean a lot pass by without acknowledgement.

Listen, I know we all have the best of intentions when it comes to saying thanks, but as life gets busy this is one of those niceties that is easily overlooked. To make sure you can express your gratitude in a timely manner, I recommend purchasing a box of thank you cards. Slip a few in your work bag so you can write letters of appreciation even when you're on the run. A hand-written note goes a long way to making people feel good about lending a helping hand.

The Encourager

The final can-do connection that needs cultivating is the one that helps you keep your sanity while staying focused on your goals. I call this person the encourager. They have a huge role in our lives, as some days they are the only one standing between you and what would be a very bad ending.

You may not call your person the encourager, but if you have one, their name will pop in your head as you read my description. This is your go-to person when stuff has hit the fan and you are so mad you can barely speak. You want to throw something, cuss people out, or start swinging, but none of those options are available to you. So, you go to your encourager to vent.

The encourager feels your pain. They listen to you for about two minutes, acknowledge your distress, and then begin to de-escalate. They don't join you in complaining or moaning. They don't hype you up so you react without thinking. Instead, they respond with encouragement, which ushers in a calmer spirit, and allows your more rational self to prevail.

God bless the encourager. For some of us, they are the only thing keeping us out of the unemployment line. On days when our mouth is too far ahead of our mind it's the encourager who helps us course correct and get back to a can-do spirit.

Does that sound like someone you know?

Perhaps the encourager is you. If so, I beseech you to take care of you. Just as you generously share your light and love with others, I want you to make sure you have someone who will pour into you.

Being the encourager is highly rewarding but it can also be utterly draining. At times, it's also isolating because your connections expect that you will always be on. Your powerful personal brand radiates positivity. So, when you are off kilter because you're tired, irritated, or simply undone by the circumstances of life people have no idea how to respond.

They often make a half-hearted attempt to try and encourage you, but really what they are most interested in is you getting back to normal so you can encourage them. And because you genuinely love affirming and inspiring other people, you bow to the pressure, pushing your own challenges to the side to help carry someone else's load.

If this is your life, here's what I want you to know.

> **Taking a time out to rest and renew your spirit is necessary self-care. It's the most effective way to ensure your gifts of affirmation and encouragement are consistently delivered with power and purpose.**

Learn to discern when you need a time out. Be unapologetic about getting still and focusing on you. Stay quiet until you are refreshed, restored, and in your right mind. Your meaningful connections will happily support your need for self-care.

If you're not the encourager, but are blessed to have one in your circle, cherish them. Be mindful that although they always appear strong, they too are human beings who experience life's ups and downs. Intentionally look for ways to express your gratitude and care for them. And when they are feeling low, extend some grace. This is a precious connection for your life and career. Make sure it is mutually beneficial.

Now if you don't have anyone like that in your life, it's probably time to expand your circle. It may be that the boundaries you've placed around yourself are too narrow. Consider taking some baby steps to reach out to your co-workers and begin to get to know them beyond just the work to be done.

One of the first things I suggest is to break the habit of eating lunch alone. Get from behind your computer and spend time with people. Even if you don't want to go out to eat, sit for a few minutes in the common areas and chat with those around you.

Make an effort to find shared points of interest and similar values. Get excited by what connects you rather than focusing on the differences often used to divide. It's amazing what you'll find when you look for reasons to like a person.

Cultivating connections takes time but they're worth it. It's the deeper relationships in our life that pay the biggest dividends.

BE BOLD, BE BRILLIANT, BE YOU

LESSON SIX

CREATE YOUR BALANCE WITH PAIN-FREE PRIORITIES

───────────

Nearly every professional woman I meet struggles with work/life balance. It makes sense when you consider that most of us have more responsibilities than we have hours in the day. Our families, careers, and communities are all important aspects of our lives. Yet we struggle to fully show up for each.

As a result, we are often riddled with guilt. Being overwhelmed, off kilter, and out of sorts becomes a daily occurrence for us. We're frustrated because we know there is a problem but we don't know how to fix it.

Well-meaning friends often tell us, "You need to find some work/life balance. You're trying to do too much."

Uh, yeah...that much is obvious. The issue is clear. It's the solution that eludes us. How in the world do we find this utopian state of work/life balance in which we are peaceful, present, and performing at our best in every area? Where's the step by step for that one?

Ladies, I've got some great news! Here's a little secret that, if you allow it, will set you free.

> There is no such thing as work/life balance. You can however, be a balanced person if you choose to live according to your priorities.

When you logically think about the notion of work/life balance it doesn't make sense. Your life is the entirety of your existence. Work is a part of it, for a specified time and season. Balancing a part of something with the whole of it will never work.

And yet we've been filled with angst over trying to reach this irrational state. Is balance possible? Sure, as long as your aim is to be a balanced person – not to balance the myriad of responsibilities that come and go.

What most of us have wrong is the mental picture of balance. We envision a woman juggling lots of different responsibilities. She's holding a baby while talking on the phone, writing in a planner, and eating lunch all at the same time. Balance for us represents being able to do all those things without dropping the ball in any area.

But that's not reality. First of all, we've already talked about why multi-tasking fuels mediocrity. Trying to keep multiple things in motion at the same time is just silliness. Second, who wants to live like that? The person in that mental picture is miserable. So, let's change the vision and then talk about how to bring it to fruition.

To become a balanced woman, we must first buy into empowered living. The graphic on the following page illustrates the dimensions that make this approach so powerful. At its essence, empowered living embraces the belief that you have the right to choose your priorities based on your values, and then exercise your authority to unapologetically live by them. It's a bold stance that puts you in the driver's seat of every aspect of your life.

This is at the heart of the women's empowerment movement I founded in 2012, *Loving on Me*. When I first began, I had one goal in mind – to help women learn to love themselves, and each other, more. In the course of my work I came to understand that changing the way we see and value ourselves is step one. Once women understood their worth, they needed practical tools to put their self-love in action. This is especially true when it comes to prioritizing our priorities.

Since the dawn of time women have worn a lot of hats, and we've done so with dignity, determination, and grace. We are fierce and loving and all together wonderful. We're also largely over committers who, even when our plate is full, will chastise ourselves for not being able to do more.

Our propensity to want to be there for everybody and everything makes it hard for us to say no. But as I and many other seasoned professionals can attest, that often comes to a bitter end. My first book opens with the story of my scary experience with anxiety and exhaustion. It is not a pretty thing when you're so determined to be there for everyone else that you lose sight of yourself.

That's why I want to give you a simple exercise to help you choose some pain-free priorities. I call them pain-free because the methodology I teach allows you to get specific and realistic. This makes it more likely that you can prioritize what's most important to you and minimize the guilt and angst that comes from missing out. These are priorities that make you, and the people you love, feel like a winner.

Let's start with listing your top *three* priorities in the box on the following page. I know some of you may struggle to only select a few, but it's important that we break the habit of thinking of everything as a priority. According to Dictionary.com, priority is defined as "something given special attention."[11]

What you're trying to identify is above all else what is most important. These should be areas that are in line with your season, values, and vision of your life. Refer back to the work we did in lesson one to ensure your responses reflect your honest desires. These highlight the "why" of what you're selecting as a priority. Aligning them ensures your priorities are what you *choose* them to be, not what you perceive they *should* be.

PRIORITIZING MY PRIORITIES		
	PRIORITY	PAIN-FREE ZONE
EXAMPLE	*My Family*	*Visit my parents at least four times a year.*
PRIORITY 1		
PRIORITY 2		
PRIORITY 3		

I've included an example to spur your thinking. "Family" is a fairly common response that I hear from both men and women when asked about their priorities. This is certainly not the case for everyone and should not be perceived as intent to influence your ranking. This is purely an illustration.

List what is most important to you. Once you have your three priorities let's work on "how" you will prioritize them. This is where we add the specificity that allows us to act. By clearly identifying what it means to us to prioritize our priorities we eliminate the ambiguity for those around us, and we release ourselves from trying to do everything and be everywhere.

This is the step that removes the pain, guilt, and anguish over constantly missing the mark. The reality is when we have priorities as big and broad as "my family" or "my career" or "my health" there are a million ways we can choose to put those first. But because we don't traditionally take a moment to determine how we're going to do so, we constantly feel like we're showing up as not enough.

> You can only achieve a goal you set.

So, let's spend a few moments focused on what success looks like when you prioritize your priorities. I'll use my example in the box to walk you through how to create your own.

My priority was "my family." My pain-free priority was to "visit my parents at least four times a year." It's actionable and achievable. Here's why it works.

First, I defined who in my family I was prioritizing. As a person who has relatives across the United States this was important. I needed to be specific so that I could prioritize without the guilt of trying to do everything and tend to everybody at once. Remember, a priority is something you give special attention. For me, that was my parents.

If your priority is your health, finances, or career, you'll likely be identifying something versus someone. For example, with a health priority you might focus on clean eating or exercise. A finance focus might be saving or reducing expenses. Really get granular so you can come up with an action plan for prioritization.

Once I decided who in my family was the priority, I thought about what I most wanted to achieve. Because my focus was people, I selected something we all could appreciate - time. However, as you know this is our most limited asset. That meant I had to come up with a realistic and achievable goal, based on my current capacity. Given my travel schedule and commitments, I estimated that was about four times a year.

When I first came up with the number of visits, I questioned if it was enough. I come from a fairly close-knit family so going months without seeing the people I love the most left me with a lot to think about. But when I stepped back and realistically looked at everything on my plate – the business, the travel, the community service, and my own self-care – I realized that was the best I could do. It was enough.

This is the kind of rational and reasoned thinking you have to apply to your priorities, too. So often it's the judgement that what we're doing is not enough that causes us so much pain. When we don't specifically define how we will prioritize, based on our resources and circumstances, we set ourselves up to constantly feel like we're lacking. The good news is that you can change that today. Let's focus on what matters most to you.

Based on your capacity, for the priorities you noted above, come up with an approach that is specific and achievable. Use the example we just walked through to take a stab at crafting your own pain-free priorities. Resist the urge to go from zero to one hundred, establishing goals that are near impossible to reach. This will set you up for failure instead of fulfillment.

We're most susceptible to doing this in areas such as our health, particularly at the beginning of the year or at pivot points in our life, such as a milestone birthday. We say things like, "I'm going to prioritize my health by eating salads for lunch and dinner six days a week."

We know when we're thinking it that it's completely unreasonable. We were eating burgers and fries four days a week last month. But because we know we should eat better we make a knee-jerk reaction that lasts for a few days at most, and then we're back to our old ways. Our priorities lay cast aside, replaced by the guilt and frustration of not putting our own needs first.

Please don't do that to yourself. Life itself presents us with so many challenges. Let's not add more to our plate by putting irrational demands on ourselves. Be kind to you by establishing some pain-free priorities that set you up for success. Then close the loop by sharing them and putting a plan in place to achieve success.

When I shared my plan with my parents to visit more often, they were elated. Knowing that seeing them was a priority for me meant the world to them. They weren't worried at all about it only being four times a year. It was enough that I was intentionally taking a break from my life to be a part of theirs.

Ladies, this is what it's like when we intentionally prioritize people. All the anxiety we feel over whether it's enough, and the guilt that tells us we should do more, is completely unnecessary. When we come up with a reasonable approach, and then share it with those we love, most often they are thrilled that we have thought enough of them to come up with a plan. It's the ambiguity that causes the angst – for us and them.

This also works when your priorities have less to do with people and more to do with self-care, your health, your finances, or your career. When you are specific you can be successful. When you plan, you can be at peace.

Let today be the last day you are living out of balance. Stop trying to do everything and instead embrace empowered living. Choose your pain-free priorities and exercise your authority to let your priorities guide your life.

I know this may seem so far out of reach, but if you implement the principles of this book in order, you'll be equipped with everything you need to succeed in creating a life and career you love. You'll also be a balanced person: full of power, peace, and infinite possibility.

BE BOLD, BE BRILLIANT, BE YOU

LESSON SEVEN

SPREAD YOUR LOVE LIKE LIFE

DEPENDS ON IT

———————

It's been an amazing journey. I hope the secrets I've shared have enriched and challenged you for the road ahead. If you've done the exercises, I have no doubt that you're ready to get in the driver's seat of your life, and career. Now I want to give you some practical advice to help you stay there.

When chatting with my tribe of busy women there are two topics that inevitably come up - self-care and service. They're not part of the competencies you traditionally think about when it comes to succeeding in your career. However, they are essential practices we need for our lives, including our career, in order to survive and thrive. Learning to love ourselves and others is the most important lesson for us to learn about living.

In the previous chapter I mentioned *Loving on Me*. We have many facets of our work, but the majority of people know us through our blog, referred to as "The Empowered Woman's Inspiration Destination." This is where a group of writers share practical advice that equips women to immediately amplify their impact. We cover a host of topics, but none more frequently than the importance of taking care of you.

> Self-care is our most important responsibility. It is a must do, so you can do the other things that you desire.

It will literally save your life, yet it's the first thing to be set aside when the demands of living overwhelm us. It's because we've learned to view self-care as a nicety, not a necessity.

We've gotten it confused with the occasional girls trip to the spa or a weekend getaway where we can check out from our normal responsibilities. While I agree those are important and definitely fun, they aren't the foundation of good self-care that leads to a happy and empowered life. If we want to be healthy – mind, body, and soul – we have to love ourselves enough to make self-care a part of our every day.

Ladies I speak from experience when I say if we leave taking care of ourselves off the list, there will eventually be an unpleasant reckoning. No matter how smart, talented, or successful we are or become this is one area where if we neglect it, we *will* come crashing down. There is no way to build and sustain a career you love without getting in the driver's seat in this area.

It's imperative, and yet often seems impossible. But it's not. All it requires is for us to be intentional, establishing healthy boundaries around what we allow into our lives, and when.

Without mentioning it directly, I've been dropping little nuggets about self-care throughout the book. I want to encapsulate them all here so you can have them at your fingertips and make a conscious choice to put them into immediate action. Here are seven things you can do, with the little time you have, to make a big difference in your day.

Set the Tone for Your Morning

We talked about setting the tone in lesson three, as a way to ensure you face the day with an attitude of gratitude. I challenged you to forget rolling over to check your phone as your first act of the day, and instead before your feet hit the floor experience a moment of gratitude. That in itself is transformative, but if you really want to amp this up, I have an even bigger challenge.

Don't touch your phone or computer for the first thirty minutes of the day.

I know for some of you, your heart beat accelerated merely from me mentioning it. You're FOMO – fear of missing out – is causing you angst even considering it. What if it's an emergency? What if someone sent an important e-mail? Shouldn't you get up to speed before you leave to go to the office?

You know there is a wonderful feature on your phone to take care of anything urgent. It rings. If there is something cataclysmic, like an alien invasion, zombie apocalypse, or a crisis at the office, they will most likely call you. So, relax and start your day stress-free.

It's amazing how peaceful you are when you can be present for the people you live with, and with your own thoughts, before any outside influences impact your mood. Stay in the driver's seat of your morning.

Cultivate Selective Ignorance

Liberate yourself from the need for real-time updates. Those of us who are old enough to remember what it was like before we had a 24/7 news cycle can assure you younger sisters that it is possible to stay informed without being obsessed. If it's really important, the news will find you. In the meantime, let's reallocate your time to where you can be productive, and still keep your peace of mind.

Focus and Finish Your Top Three

We've already talked about the damage multi-tasking can do. Yet we continue to do it because it gives us the illusion of getting more done in less time. In truth what's really happening is that you are doing a bunch of stuff mediocrely, and mastering none.

Change the game by committing to excellence. Reduce your stress by focusing on less. Start by identifying your top three to-do each day, and then begin with what's *most* important first. If you resist the urge to add more to your list, you'll be amazed how much you accomplish and how well it will be done, simply by giving yourself permission to pay attention.

Schedule Joy Breaks

In lesson three I also mentioned the importance of scheduling joy breaks. When life is full to overflowing, identifying those little things you can do each day to decompress can make a world of difference. Calling a friend, playing with our pets, or taking a short walk outside can boost your mood, and give you fresh energy to finish the day. The key is to add those fifteen minute breaks to your calendar and stick with them. Renewing your spirit is essential for maintaining your balance.

Stop Unnecessary Speech

Someone once told me, "You will never win an argument you shouldn't be having." When you think about how much energy most of us waste in conversations to nowhere, you can see how essential learning how to stop talking is to your self-care. Protect your mind from the chaos that comes from arguing, and instead, be more selective about how and when you speak.

Embrace an Evening Ritual

Often our evenings are so full there's no clear end to our day. It's as if we're on all the time, and as a result, our bodies and minds never get a signal that it's time to slow down and relax. That's why it's important to develop a repetitive way to close out your day.

For me, it's those few precious moments every night when I'm taking off my make-up. As I cleanse my face and rub on my moisturizer, I spend a little time loving on me. I intentionally slow myself down so I can enjoy the experience, closing out my work day the same way I begin, by giving thanks.

What evening ritual can you develop to send your body the signal it needs to close your day in a positive way?

Steep Yourself in Sleep

It's recommended that women over the age of eighteen get seven to nine hours of sleep each night, yet most of us get far less. Pregnancy, menopause, a medical condition or stress can all cause temporary interruptions in our sleep. If you're currently experiencing any of those, please talk to your doctor about how to ensure you can get your proper rest.

In the meantime, here are some practical home remedies you can try to help ease you into a relaxed, and sleep-ready, state.

- ✓ First, let the phone charge in the kitchen rather than by your bed. The lights and sounds of your phone are all designed to attract your attention which will distract you from sleeping.

- ✓ Second, avoid caffeine and sugary foods too close to bedtime. It counters the effect of your evening ritual and pumps you up with fake energy that will keep you awake.

- ✓ Third, turn the television off or better yet, take the TV out of your bedroom. Create a sanctuary that is reminiscent of the spa and designed to support your rest.

- ✓ Finally, stick to a regular sleep schedule. Condition your body to seek out slumber by giving yourself a bedtime. The more consistent you are the easier it will be to get to sleep.

Making self-care an everyday intention will make you stronger, more resilient, and infinitely more productive. This is your key to longevity, and coupled with your priorities, your sanity. Love you enough to make choices that are in your own best interest. This will ensure that you are powered up, and can passionately love others, through service.

In her book *The Measure of Our Success,* Marian Wright Edelman wrote, "Service is the rent we pay for living. It is the very purpose of life, and not something you do in your spare time." It's in a chapter where she talks about her family's legacy of service, and how it shaped her as a human being. What's interesting is how serving with her family also shaped her self-worth.

During a time when segregation was the norm in America, her community serving each other, created a positive narrative around the value of black children. They learned that the "measure of our worth was inside our head and heart, not outside in our possessions or on our backs." She was taught by example that no matter who you are, or how much you had, everyone had something to give.

Service was the key to significance.

As we think about how to create a career we love, service must be at the heart of it. Indeed, it is central to our lives. For it is in embracing a spirit of service that we unlock our life's greatest work.

The beautiful part is we do not have to do a certain type of work to serve. While I've spent a great deal of my career as a senior leader within not-for-profit organizations, it was actually my work at the oil and gas company that really crystallized my thinking in this area.

I was a Royalty Analyst, a small cog in the wheel of a very large multi-layered organization. My work booking oil and gas revenues was fairly repetitious, which was part of what eventually led to the discontent I mentioned in lesson one. However, there was one thing about my position that was really fulfilling.

The wells for which I was responsible for booking revenue were on Native American lands. For some tribes, it was their largest source of revenue. They needed these resources to provide for their communities, and their cause became my "why."

Yes, my work was for the company. But in doing it to the best of my ability, I was also benefitting the tribes. I didn't love the work, but when put in proper perspective, I could still see it as significant. In my own way, I was serving.

This is the perspective we all can apply to the work we do everyday.

> Service is what makes life sweet, and your living significant.

We don't have to do mission trips in developing lands, or work full-time at a non-profit, to contribute in profound ways to the world around us. Right where we are, with what's in front of us, there is meaningful work for us to do. It is to spread love by serving.

Sometimes the missing element to creating a career we love is our mindset. We go to work every day and do the work, but forget that no matter what our task, at the end of the day we are serving the needs of people. Even if you never get a chance to see the person at the end, they should be your "why," motivating you to bring your best self to each task.

I have met women who embrace this mindset across nearly every sector. From the sanitation worker who cleans up the bathroom, to the CEO who is mentoring other young leaders, they have identified the value of what they are doing for others, and it changes their whole countenance. This is my hope for you, too. Because until you feel good about your contribution at the office, it doesn't matter if you're in the right role, you won't enjoy the work.

Of course, it's still important for us to volunteer our time and talent in meaningful ways that address issues affecting our entire community. By all means, join with your friends and families to volunteer and fundraise for your favorite charities. Just don't position those activities as the only way you serve.

For most of us, that is a small but significant part of our lives that we can activate just a few times a year. If that's the only time you think about service you will consistently feel as though your life is lacking some significant part. Your work – where you spend the bulk of your time each day – must be viewed as service, in order to fill the hole, you feel in your life.

Embrace service to unlock your significance. When you identify the "why" for your work, you will dramatically increase your job satisfaction. You'll also begin to love the life you have designed. There's nothing like serving others to remind you of your purpose, value, and worth.

THE ROAD AHEAD

As we close out our journey together, I want to leave you with a few parting words of encouragement. First and foremost, you are an amazing soul designed for unimaginable success. Your past does not define you, nor do your present circumstances confine you. Life is full of infinite possibilities. When you believe in you, fields of opportunity begin to bloom.

Throughout our journey, my goal has been to help you become intimately familiar with your greatness. Knowing who you are, and understanding your worth, are critical to creating a life that is tailor-made for your divine design. If you haven't done the exercises in lessons one and two, I encourage you to go back and do the work.

Your unstoppable superpower is waiting to be activated. And when you do, life as you know it will never be the same.

The power of unleashing your whole self, allowing your brilliance to shine bright, is both liberating and elevating. Not just for you, but for everyone around you, as you use your light to ignite others. This is your purpose, and your destiny.

As career women we have so much to give. We are strong leaders who know how to get things done. When we're balanced and empowered, there is no stopping us.

The key is for us to stay flexible, alert, and ready. Lesson three and four help you get prepared and in position. The principles featured in the book are not magic, but they will help you make bold moves. Really spend some time thinking about areas where you need to up your game, and then put an action plan in place to make it happen.

Remember, most every decision affecting your career is made "behind the closed door." Just because you don't know about an opportunity doesn't mean that it doesn't exist. Embrace a spirt of abundance and stay expectant. The best careers are often made up of what seem like random occurrences. But when they are viewed over time, you can clearly see that the stops that seemingly had little value, were always a part of the divine design.

Every experience is part of the beautiful puzzle that makes our life's masterpiece.

So, don't plan to go it alone. Very often it's other people who add critical pieces to our puzzle. Every time we make a move it creates a shift in the atmosphere, and our ripples go far and wide.

Your hopes and dreams inspire those of others. Your boldness causes more women to stand strong. When you are vulnerable enough to be authentic, you liberate others from their self-imposed limits.

Your success produces seeds that grow into opportunities for others.

Make sure that your connections are strong, and your priorities are in order. People are life's most precious gift. Treasure those you love and be good to those who need our help. We must never get too busy to see and serve those in need.

Finally, above all else, take care of you. I've tried the whole "work myself into the ground plan," and I can confirm it does not work. Self-awareness and self-care

are critical for achieving career success. Make it your mission to love you, and those around you, like your life depends on it. Believe it or not, it really does.

Completing the exercises contained in the book will help you identify and take your natural next step. Focus so you can finish strong. Our most limited assets – time and energy – should only be invested in people, places, and things that will yield a great return.

As you continue on your journey, I want to make sure you're surrounded with the additional tools and resources you'll need to succeed. Through *Loving on Me* and our Academy we offer courses, coaching, and community. It's a system designed to affirm your worth, and to activate your expertise in ways that allow you to immediately amplify your impact.

Visit me on line at **katrinamcghee.com** to access more resources.

While there you can also join our empowered executive tribe. We're committed to creating the lives we want to live, while being balanced, and building vibrant careers. For daily inspiration, join us on social media. We work hard to be a positive force for good, encouraging each other to believe in ourselves and to be our best. It's a great place to begin building a network of like-minded people, with whom at some point, you may want to build a deeper connection.

Ladies, it's time to get in the driver's seat, and head on down the road. I wish you safety, success, and significance on your journey. Choose happiness each day and be unafraid to drive right on past the lines of your comfort zone. There is a land of adventure waiting beyond what you know. Go get your more.

What you have been created to accomplish, you have been equipped to achieve. You have within everything you need to succeed.

Be Bold. Be Brilliant. Be You.

BE BOLD, BE BRILLIANT, BE YOU

ABOUT THE AUTHOR

Katrina McGhee is an author, speaker, and career success strategist. For over twenty years, she served as a senior executive for two of the world's most recognizable non-profits, revolutionizing the way women were ignited to take charge of their health. Realigning her knowledge and experience of inspiring wellness, Katrina now serves as a women's empowerment advocate, inspirational leader, and a corporate trainer.

In 2012, Katrina launched *Loving on Me*, a global movement encouraging women to love themselves and each other more. Through her website, books, videos, and thriving social community, thousands of women have joined her tribe.

Katrina is passionate about helping people reach their highest heights. With years of business experience, she is uniquely skilled at igniting change at individual and corporate levels in leadership, personal branding and career development. Through her *Loving on Me Academy*, she provides online courses that empower audacious women to lead, inspire, and succeed.

Whether Katrina is transforming a corporate culture or inspiring individuals to achieve unimaginable success, McGhee is a powerful agent of change.

MORE BY KATRINA MCGHEE

What Do You Do When You Don't Know What to Do, But You Know It's Time to Do Something Different?

Loving on Me! Lessons Learned on the Journey from MESS to MESSAGE reveals the steps you can take to break free from the status quo for good. Through a series of powerful life lessons inspired by Katrina's personal journey of transformation, you'll discover how to get more out of life than just going through the motions, and be ignited to live fully, completely, and abundantly.

For more visit katrinamcghee.com.

ENDNOTES

---

[1] https://news.gallup.com/opinion/chairman/212045/world-broken-workplace.aspx

[2] https://womenintheworkplace.com/

[3] https://news.starbucks.com/news/starbucks-pay-equity-for-partners

[4] https://en.wikipedia.org/wiki/Personal_branding

[5] https://www.talentinnovation.org/assets/ExecutivePresence-KeyFindings-CTI.pdf

[6] https://www.talentinnovation.org/assets/ExecutivePresence-KeyFindings-CTI.pdf

[7] https://www.thriveglobal.com/stories/46944-9-ways-multitasking-is-killing-your-brain-and-productivity-according-to-neuroscientists?utm_source=LinkedIn&utm_medium=Arianna

[8] https://magneticspeaking.com/7-unbelievable-fear-of-public-speaking-statistics/

[9] https://www.inc.com/carmine-gallo/the-one-skill-warren-buffett-says-will-raise-your-value-by-50.html

[10] https://www.medicaldaily.com/why-using-pen-and-paper-not-laptops-boosts-memory-writing-notes-helps-recall-concepts-ability-268770

[11] https://www.dictionary.com/browse/priority

33646309R00088

Made in the USA
Middletown, DE
18 January 2019